SIXTEEN

SIXTEEN

A Compilation of Poems

Amie Woleslagle

Copyright © 2022 by Amie Woleslagle

Cover design by Abigail Daniels @graphics_by_gracie

All rights reserved. No part of this publication may be reproduced, distributed, or transmitted in any form or by any means, including photocopying, recording, or other electronic or mechanical methods, without the prior written permission of the publisher, except in the case of brief quotations embodied in critical reviews and certain other noncommercial uses permitted by copyright law.

Pixy Publishing
Printed in the United States of America
First Printing, 2022
ISBN 9781735636924

www.AmieWoleslagle.com

To Hannah F
Death might have claimed you as his own
But it's only a stop on the eternal road

& To those who lit
Injustice's fuse
May the fire burn
And never burn you.

Overture

I breathed and was gone . . .

I blinked and was lost . . .

I spoke but nothing was heard . . .

Because I survived in a

vacuum.

She turned sixteen that fateful year
The year she could not find relief
She tossed and turned to lie just right
To find a promised release.

There once was a girl
Who wrote life's lessons
Down in a notebook
Some in poetry, some in prose
She opened her heart for others to know
Published a collection but wasn't through
Now she writes another for you,
Introducing her problems to reality.

1

Amber Gold

I have a problem.
I don't know me
I haven't been introduced
You see.

The pressure builds
Preserving my soul
In amber liquid shimmering gold.

Choking on unfiltered air
Burning in this atmosphere
My mold is set, I am in place

Pain the result of truth
Love given when I lie
What they don't know is that this is how I die.

Death is a sweet relief
It introduces me to me
It reveals all the unseen
It gives me undying relief.

Her thoughts are louder
Than all the sounds around
The graveyard of hopes and buried dreams
Her reality continues to be.

 # 2

Echoes

Do you hear the echoes

Bouncing off the walls?

Do you hear the echoes

Of nothing at all?

Can you claim the echoes

Of chaos all around?

Can you claim the echoes

Before they bury me under ground?

To hide behind a role
Is much easier for her
Than to face time's tragic truth
She is a coward and a child
Running from another hour
Where hurt her soul will be
Infection trickles in the wound
All because fear is her master
And she has yet to harness her own power.

 # 3

Revolving

My mind is a revolving door
Whining as faces fly before
Let me hide behind its walls
Let me cling before I fall.

Wishing wells cannot heal my mind,
They will only buy me time
Capsules swallowed as I retreat
Waiting for loved ones to release.

My mind is a revolving door
Emotions flicker right before
Personalities switch to and fro
Each one in pain because of the whole.

Pencil lead snaps when her eyes find her plight
She is never going to be anything if she does
not fight.

4

Desecration

My head slams against the wall,
My voice echoes with the thunder of it all
As I am in solitary confinement
I am a dead man chained to a casket.

My feet slip and sink into mud,
My fingers are one with the sky above,
I am a prisoner of war,
I am a field battle torn.

My breath freezes and dissipates,
My chest is a furnace of emotions and hate,
I am a forest fire,
I am the Alaskan wilds.

My screams echos in empty caverns
My whispers resound, crashing on waves
I am depression as a human
I am the individual you've come to hate.

My heart patterns in time with the rain
My blood leaks and mars the floor,

I am a magma chamber beneath the surface,
I am the desecration Tokyo witnessed.

```
              Time is no man's friend and yet
               To our heroine it is a safety net
               To keep her from the scorching sun
          Even if it locked her beneath earth's crust.
```

 # 5

7:01

7:01 I'm alive, I feel the sun
        I blink
7:02 I've sunk beneath the crust
Control lost in the utter rush
Of the unexplored.

7:34 memories left uneasily
        I breathe
And time has run out.
7:35 the known has shifted & grown
Now I'll never really know me.

8:02 What did I do
        Questions arrest me
8:03 I'll never actually be free
Caught between the core and crust
Magma burning my skin to rust.

9:35 begs the question who am I
        I sneeze
Identity is captured in cryo freeze
9:36 the universe might spit
Out someone a little bit like me.

Eons in place, searching through space
        I'm no longer me

Millions of minutes maybe I'll win it eventually
Be the creation of science intermittently.

If only time wasn't a camera and I wasn't its mode dial
The shutter wouldn't fall and capture us all
In time's mortal grip.
Shy smile on time's hand
It tips just enough for me to understand


```
                Climb, breaking, tearing free
             Stress and health are on a degree
            Each one trying to balance the other
          Which one will win is a question for another
```

Unnormality

I can't breathe
It shouldn't be normal
But it is for me.

I can't see
Without my head spinning
And my heart hurting beneath me.

I can't think
Without chasing trains
And random unrelated strains.

It shouldn't be normal
My soul shouldn't strain
All to keep from the drain.

I can't hear
Without voices taunting
And hatred dripping.

I can't smell
Without sniffing chemicals

Wafting and making me unwell.

I can't taste
Without toxicity burning
My lips pursing.

It shouldn't be normal
But what in this world
 is as it should?

It shouldn't be normal
But I catch the butterflies, understanding normal
Is no fun.

It shouldn't be normal
But then again what's life
Without the chaos of

Unnormality.

```
      An hour where there's no calamity
        Where she doesn't point it out
             Asking someone to see
            Someone to notice and agree
   This life is a heavy burden called reality.
```

 # 7

What I See

Do you see the world like me?
Do you see the smile refrained?
Do you see the beauty of dirt?
Do you see neglected melodies?

Do you hear the sounds like me?
The never ending tears?
The silent cries and fears
Or the song death whispers near?

Do you smell the world like me?
The brimstone burning the great sea?
The fragrant notes of lavender
Or the bitter scent of humanity?

Do you taste the world like me?
Bitter from the curse, I believe.
And yet the taste can shift and change
From mellow to bold in a single phrase.

Does the world feel the same
To you and to me?

Can you touch sorrow and feel the pain
Your stomach twisting all the same?

Or am I the only one with senses?
The only one with temptations
To scream into the deep abyss
And ask the gods to grant one gift?

The gift to give others what I see.


```
              As she takes stock of her life
           The common denominator in this strife
                 Is the fact that she's alive
              In all her relationships it could be
         Her who creates the tension and calamity.
            At least, people have told her in heat
               To blame herself for how they treat
                    The person inside her frame.
```

 # 8

The Problem

The problem is I hate life,
I hate the pain,
The incessant drone
Of voices inside.

I hate wanting something new,
I hate how each thing I say
Isn't exactly true.

I hate that I know no one,
I hate my glass cage.
I hate existence
In this mercenary age.

My poetry is all about my needs
Beginning with I
And ending with me
Is that why I have so many insecurities?

Or is my problem
Simple, blatant distaste?
My tears have gone missing,

My sobs have ceased.

But the ache in my heart
Has failed to relieve.

People say patience
Will heal my ill.
People claim time
Will turn back its till.

But the sun rises
And it sets
And it does so again,
But the pain does not ease.


```
         To be enough is her simply goal
         She is killing herself to bestow
          Perfection to those she loves
              To be what they created
              To be what they all needed
        More than the girl she is inside.
```

9

Persecution

Exhaustion s
             i
                  n
                       k
                            s into my mind
Delusions chat all at one time
Pain rotates on a golden platter
Shushing all that really matters.

Preparation couldn't ready me this time
Depression clouds all that's mine
Allergies suck energy from my bones
Drowning all desires in droves.

Persecution is a word to use
Deliverance isn't a thing I choose
Hard work pushes my exhausted soul
Until I've driven myself into a hole.

Wringing my heart in two,
Serve it with whatever tool.
Wipe the smile off my corpse's face,

You'll find p
        a
            i
                    n in its place.

```
Did they think they could beat out her soul?
Perhaps it'll come and bite them in droves
    Temper awakened, backbone replaced
  Maybe our girl will storm down the gates.
```

 # 10

Insane

Lying lips and a burning tongue
Heart on fire, melting this one.

Vibrant eyes, crimson lips
Blood stains mar whiter hints

Heart beats in time to a mortal drum
But even the tempo isn't enough.

Cleanse my mind, it's dirty stuff
Burn my heart until it's tough.

Lies chase each thought above
Hiding every ounce of love.

Who is right, am I wrong?
I am lost in this noisy throng.

Heart and mind battle the pain
They forget our earthly name.

Help is offered by its countenance slowed

Hope held out but I'm already through.

Hunger messes with my brain
Spasms shudder through my frame.

Lies, lies they cover my name
Lies, lies, are they sane?

Or am I completely insane?

```
        Armed with a pen and words galore
          Our heroine pounds on your door
            To deliver a glorious gift
           Camaraderie and hope to shift
       Your thoughts of death and of revenge.
```

11

Copyright

Morbid though my thoughts may be
My soul can find any kind of ecstasy

Words grow together into a tree
So others may see my morbidity

But my soul is not so complete
For death to own it's total seat

I may very well hear it's pipes
But I have not given it my copyright.

The world is brighter due to shadows
By mind is keener due to the shallows

And so I smile in spite of the dark
Just to show others that they too can start.

The war avoided she turns her eyes
She knows there are moments in history
That define a single age
All have lived through at least one
Some more than they can say
The year she started this isolation
Drifted by unchanged
Her soul was burned, burning
Crafted into a new shape.

12

Pandemonium

Eternity of Isolation here we come
Moments of remembering never are
A welcome chink to the armor we hold
Darkness is closer than we were told.
Like the rearview mirror, it appears to be
Farther than in reality and yet we still are tied
To our houses as others pass away
Masks hide our features, our breath is warm
Keeping frostbite from nipping our tongue
Cough in public, you'll be damned
Tarnation is enough for that evil man
Pace the house back and forth
Tiger King is no more
Pace the house back and forth
Perhaps the Lord with allow new birth
Outside the sun continues to rise and set
But you've had enough of your family's bet
Each of them never more than a few feet away
Why don't they find their own way of coping today?
Eternity of Isolation, here we come
We give up on the hope of salvation for everyone
The vaccine is on hold and so are our lives

Maybe this could actually be nice
If we weren't a tiger, pacing back and forth
Staring at the television that shows us south from north
Normality still portrayed in the most boring of shows
And that is how insanity slows
Eternity of Isolation
Here we come
Please let me survive
Let us all survive
As one.


```
            Different, yet always the same
             Watching the clock creep away
             Her morbid thoughts on display
          Our girl chants as her pen begins
         To immortalize the clock's renegade.
```

 # 13

The Clock

Tick Tock
Ignore the clock
Tick Tock
Pleasure stops.
 Tick Tock
Life goes on
Tick Tock
Make it stop
Tick Tock
Hold your pen
Tick Tock
Quick begin
Tick Tock
Mark your word
Tick Tock
Never stop
Tick Tock
Time is done
Tick Tock
Death has begun
Tick Tock
Stutter away
Tick Tock

Your end is today.

```
           It's incessant ticking is a blade,
             Why put faith in that blade?
         Why believe in a blade that is designed to cut?
             Why follow liars into their hut?
               Rebellion fills the air today
         Our heroine knows what she believes but to pray
              To the same God her enemies use
           Seems like bowing to their abusive tunes.
```

14

The Way of Destruction

The way of destruction
Clothed in hope
My soul cries for it
And clings to a rope

Parched, my tongue longs for water
But wine is poured and I drown.

The way of destruction
Is a raft
My hands grip to it
And collapse.

Bleeding, a waterfall is on the way
Salt tied into it, capping the sway.

The way of destruction
Is crystal clear
And my body is on it
I'm bound for there.

So she searches for something else
Safety appears and floods her mind
It's a gem of great price
It isn't found in holiness's pike
But maybe religion isn't a form
Maybe it's a relationship that's been torn.

 # 15

Pyxis

Hours and hours
Tick by, balanced on an ace,
But my heart hasn't found
Safety's interval of space.

Perhaps it's waiting
Underneath a stone
Perhaps it's calling
A siren's verse to its own.

My soul echoes in infinity
Seeking absence of that peace
I know it's there, under the scenes
Pyxis will point me to the answer of my needs.

The direction is hardly ever clear
And that's why my tears remain here
But let me have a taste of peaceful pie
Allow me to go to heaven this time.

With all this swarming in her mind,
The girl who pens these depressing letters
Tried again to end it with these meters
But the gift of life is too sweet
For her to give up simply for free.

 # 16

Relief

Drama drama fills my head
Lilting melodies replace the dead.

Poems ripped from a bleeding heart
Where did this tragedy all start?

Whispered prayers scream into a void
Muted agonies answer questions toyed.

But inside the cymbals are a ploy
To hide the trauma underneath joy.

Music slams my ear drums in defense
Rewinding my mind to make sense.

Trauma trauma changes my mind
Moments continue to forever rewind.

Nightmares taunt me in the darkness
Sleep is a luxury I have failed to harness.

Muscle tension rules as I fight the tics

My mind forgets all my heart's nicks.

Wounded soul will never have a break
In this life unless I decide to take

Life to find relief.

```
         In response to her own lies
       She wrote this to conquer minds
  To show them the truth instead of the lies.
```

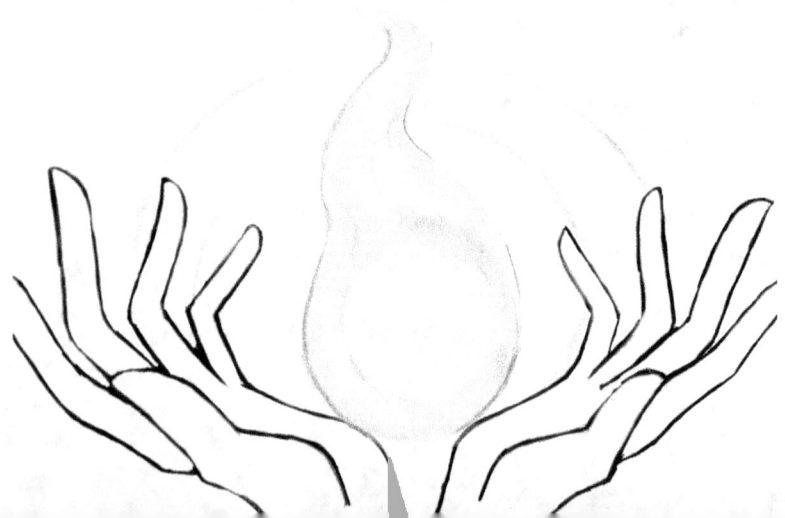

17

It's Tricky

It's tricky
They said
To catch a sunbeam
    It's impossible
        They said
To find a smile
    It's tiring
        They said
To be an angel
So they visited with the devil instead.

    It's tricky
        I said
To climb out a rabbit hole
    It's impossible
        I said
To give up.
    It's tiring
        I said
But oh so worth it
Which is why I'm not dead.

When she told them of her pain,
They whispered around her all the same
How many people asked her to sit tight?
How many times did she wonder if it was right
And fair to be captured here
When all her mind knew was pain.

 # 18

Alive

Death whispered in my ear,
Darkness hovered, waiting to hear

You shouted, and grabbed my hand
Your tears burned as the blood ran.

Your words were muted as fingers twitch
Every inch screams, fighting against the itch.

You say to stay, you look at me across a screen
You ask me to tell you, but I can barely stand being seen.

Every moment is a fight I feel as if I'm losing
Conquered ground

Your concern is empty, burning like liquid nitrate
My heartbeat slows as I try to concentrate.

Your concerns aren't worth crying,
My mental health is dying.

Death extends a bony hand,

Its eyes are black, its visage grim

And yet my heart isn't human in its fear,
I hasten my end, clawing it near.

Your eyes are in my mind, staying my hand
Your prayers hover around, forming a protective band.

I may cry for death, but it is not mine
Life lays claim to me and I am still alive.

```
      People asks if she wants immortality
         But she craves death and peace
          Not the same never ending fight
             Watching all she loves die.
          If people could just meet death
       Maybe they wouldn't fear it's breath
             They'd see what she sees
                An undisturbed knife.
```

 # 19

Knife

Mysterious to the beings of life
Bringing light to all kinds of strife
The passage from the present to the future life
Death is . . . an undisturbed knife.

Sharpened by each passing iron
The blade will steal a humans entire
View of reality if not their heart beat
And yet it is not a thief.

No, death is considered a wonderful thing
Its silence, its presence, humanity spends moments
Viewing it with either longing or fear
There is no immortality here.

But days slide by, and she still lives
Our heroine meets new and different people
Questioned about who she is
She's without an answer.
She knows she's a nobody
A toy others play with for eternity
While others looked pained at her response
She finds freedom in her lot
To be a ghost is relieving.

20

Identity

I am nobody
My worth is gone
I am nobody
The world moves on

Each person wants to be somebody
I am not one
Everyone is a somebody
But I have won.

I am a nobody
A shadow of a skull
I am a nobody
A human soul.

You are a somebody
The world presses close
You are a somebody
But don't you know?

I am nobody.
A simple soul.

I am nobody
A worthless bibliopole.

I love being nobody
A whirl o' a wisp.
I am nobody,
A mystery in the mist.

```
          A ghost with no connection
         A ghoul with nothing but the wind
          She puts on her mask and smiles
               Hiding the hurt within
              But if all are happy
               All is well within
          Because who is she but a slave
                To everyone's whims.
```

21

Nicety

Scalding hot in its burn
Chillingly cold in the way it goes
Lukewarm, the breath against my cheek
The wind is the only thing that loves me.

Dye changing it to a different hue
Accents chosen by you know who
Holes hidden too far for perfection to reach
Only the seamstress really sees me.

Changing shoes to fit your pain,
Rearranging my hair today
Empty inside but too vibrant to see
I am fake, an unreal nicety.

The only place she can hide
Is in the written script
So she disappears for hours at a time
To relish and live inside a book.

22

Literary Tome

At times I cannot bear to live,
I find a pool in which I swim,
Inky letter swirl and pull me in
Gentle pages touch my lips.

Adventures swirl in crimson stains
The images filter and still remain
My perspective rotates and continues to change
When I examine a book.

Worlds with new ideas fill my mind
Constraints aren't known in adventure this time
Every breath reminds me what is mine,
Mine for all the keeping.

Would that I could enter the tide
Would that the black world all combine
So I can forget all the times
Reality was too bitter to continue without dreams.

Books bring relief, adventures, peace
Books ease the ache in my soul

Placing experiences and adding to tales untold
Books are the way I show

Love, attention, attraction, and grief
Feelings others won't let me release
Books are the way I display my woes
As with stories I grow

Books are a way we communicate
With the dead who have meditated
The world in which hate torrents
The world in which we live.

Books are my relief
Take a moment to breathe
Leather on my cheek
My mind in another world.

                        And she finds
That despite all in life refusing respite
    Something creeps in her soul
    Nose in a book, hope comes to look
   And change her mindset as a whole.

23

Free Rein

Strange substance in my soul
Redecorating and making it home
Perhaps I should call for it to stop
But my soul is not used to work.

Light appears, dust particles rain
They've opened the blinds and made it day
It has banished depression and made life stay
I'm awakened in this new way.

Let it awake you, restore your soul
Let it give your reasons to survive it all
Let it whisper, let it scream
Give it what it asks for, free rein.

Different perch to watch the battle
Her mind is the battleground
Who will win this awful war
And who will be buried aground?

24

Mind's Ride

Stable, stable
The cornerstone wobbles
Mental, mental,
My mind is a stable.

Horses, horses,
Their noise comes in torrents.
Thunder, thunder,
It doesn't silence my hunger.

Silence, silence,
They tell my lips to cease.
Mental, mental,
We're all falling to some degree.

Fake it, fake it,
A stone mask in place.
Break it, break it,
I need to see my face.

Blood, blood,
It creates a sea.

Pulse, pulse,
The moments pass unendingly.

Wash, wash,
My ivory skin revealed.
Whimper, whimper
The blood hasn't healed.

Stable, stable,
That is not my name.
Mental, mental,
That is the devil's game.

Horses, horses,
My legs outstretch to run.
Thunder, thunder,
I have loaded my guns.

```
        Though the battle wages
          She can't stop her work
        Foot in front of the other
          Though her muscles shook.
The next best thing is all she can do,
       The guns fire a loud salute
      As the tears stay in her eyes
       And she continues her climb.
```

25

The Next Best Thing

Is that all life is
The next best thing?
Heart racing
Mind praying
But it's just the next best thing

My muscles tremble
At the memories missing
Skin prickles
Eyes wiggle
And I'm doing the next best thing.

Keep on keeping on
Is what they all say
I'm done
It's overrun
The next best thing.

Patience isn't my virtue
And pain is in control of my curfew
Heart beat
It stinks

The next best thing.

```
Finding shelter in the ivory tower
 It echoes gunshots by the hour
 Our heroine has no where to go
 But at least she calls it home.
```

26

Glass Dome

Will the ringing never stop
Will the drone forever go on?
Will my eyes continue to weep
While Earth rests in her seat?

Will you never wipe my tears
Or does my sorrow continue to scare
All the humans from my sight
Leaving me alone each night?

My ears have lost the tune tonight
No longer do I strive to be right
So my world is a glass dome
At least I have my own home.

In the tower all she has to do
Is go through her thoughts
All her life she heard the stories
Of the god who a kingdom glories
But he doesn't answer her cries
And when he does it is to numb the surprise

 # 27

Liquor

There is a creator I absolutely hate
His creations made of clay
Each spin of the wheel turmoils my soul
Each broken vessel destroys

I have a single request for the creator of clay
A simple request for him to answer
I prayed every day asking for death
Instead he gave me liquor.

He has cathedrals painted with pictures high
Judgement crowning this one guy
An inflated figure of a man
Scared her more than you can understand.

 # 28

Torture My Belief

He uses plaster to bind the wound
In the same movement he cuts anew.
Blood coats his hand as he simply says
Love made me do it again.

There is a creator I simply cannot know
He creates with clay and shapes to show
That cracks are created by his willing hand
And with the same hand he fixes our brands.

His love is something I cannot know
It slathers on salve and breathes poison in its hole
He whispers promises of great relief
And yet he continues to torture my belief.

He is something I cannot understand
My heart falters when I see His hand
A great judge sitting on his throne
Him will I ever really own?

But the image isn't true
She's introduced to something new
A Captain of the sea
A man who values personality
Who's pain for her is greater than his own
A man who gives her peace and love.

29

Sailor's Storm

Sailor's storm brews afar
Captain's eyes assure us all
Port bow blows the wind
A few promising our course to stall

Nautical nets entwine my heart
My captain's fingers tear apart
Rope after rope falls to the floor
He knows all that we are.

Light house embers on my grave
Signify the light that shown on my life
Heaven is a home that grow brighter each day
The light on the past lends music to the fyfe.

Elements fight the image of God
Habits bring back the hardened heart
Can she have a new start?

 # 30

Hail

Hail

The storm to beat us

Lightning

The electricity to kill us

God

The man with the hammer on the throne

God

A being that demands justice alone.

They say he could see all the earth
He planned all her pain on a graphic stage
And ignored her cries as it continued to play
What kind of God does that?

 # 31

Mega Screen

Before God my life has unplayed
On the mega screen He has made
Eating popcorn as I fall to my feet
What kind of God makes and creates
Only to punish and cripple and break
Enjoying the hidden landmines beneath
The feet of the children he promised to bequeath.

So our heroine turns her eyes
Away from the faith full of lies
But she realized to recant
She'd have to destroy a part of herself.

32

White Board

Agnostic
A hypocrite of the highest form
Should I recant
All I've said and done before?

Life is not a white board
There is no way to erase
My words and my convictions
Without a slap to my face.

Written in blood
With time's signature applied
My words are nothing
I can erase or hide.

Agnostic
A hypocrite of the highest form
I can't recant or change
All I've said and done before.

In that darkest hour
Where the pain was mental forever
Angels came to her sweet relief
Sent from the Captain of the Seas.

33

Ministry

Angels minister to me,
Giving me their energy.
My heartbeat quickens
With darkness slightly eloquent.
Oh my mind is rotating
Into nothingness
As I try to remember
God's amazingness.

Laying still, the questions poured
From the wound out to the Lord
Questions no one wanted to hear
But the Captain turned his ear

 # 34

Virtue

What does faith mean to you?
What mysteries do you swim through?

When the sun sets, where does it go?
When will we all die, do you know?

Why do we stand and yet fall so hard?
Why do we fear and still become charred?

Where do we drift when we have no faith?
Where do we lay when we're put in the grave?

How do we test and review our own soul?
How do we smile when there's things we don't know?

My soul is breaking, torn in two,
My heart is crumbling as I fight for you.

You are religion, my only virtue.
Yet you don't know what faith means to you.

Pain is strange, it pulls back the blinds
Though she had not answers she'd choose
She helps others in doubts through
Because her eyes had been blessed to see
Beauty in humanity.

35

Telescope

I have a telescope
Into a person's soul
I have a telescope
Made of pure gold

I trace the constellations
Of a person's mind
I trust my gut
Every single time.

Wrinkle in the heavenly host
A forgotten scar at their throat
My telescope sees and understands
I am not a judge, just a helping hand.

I have a telescope
Into a person's heart
I have a telescope
To view their work of art.

Humanity is not a blinder
It is a magnify glass and a reminder
Of the chaos in her head
Of all the discomfort in her bed.

36

Phantom

I have a phantom following me
A train of thoughts I cannot think

Violet the hue that haunts my dream
Lavender whispers of monarchy

Flat and sharp, the melody twinkles
It continues its sound in a minor key

Gentle the scent of lilac seas
It cannot truly banish my unease

Mist on my fingers gathers dew droplets
Chasing the grooves my skin has furrowed

Academic dreams dwell with eggnog taste,
Perhaps it's why I continue my chase

Onward and onward toward higher ground
Satan tempts me to throw myself down

But my soul refuses to leave,

I step toward the temple doors

Will the phantom follow me
Or shall I be truly free?

Deadbolt drawn, oaken wood strong,
I take one last look before I fall

Bidding my phantom a good life beyond.


```
        Scales fall and hearts bleed
         But religion has many keys
       Some are iron in their compound
      But some are made of heart and flesh.
```

 # 37

Contamination

Unanswered letters twirl through my mind
Begging attention and adventures to find
Worlds of questions a mile wide
Blocking faith and covering mine.

Flickering fire tempts to burn
Paper scraps fill the urn
My confusion a rising cloud of smoke
Covering and contaminating all I know.

Whisper, whisper to clear my mind
Water, water, wash and find
Clear all that keeps my from my own
Show me religion and the great unknown.

With religion still in dispute
Her eyes continue to search the lives of men
Stupid though the mortals be
They show up again and again.

 # 38

Groundhog Day

Sin is like groundhog day
The repetition of all you say
Lie after lie paints your mind
Pleasure is actually hard to find.

Sin is like a carousel
Moving and moving all involved
But the view will never change
Because it's simply groundhog day.

Sin is like a merry-go-round
Laughter spinning till you hit the ground
Air is gone as pain remains
Wickedness is always paid.

Just desserts on a plate laid
Sour sends tastebuds want away
Sin will catch you one of these days
But, of course, continue in your ways.

Eyes on others, she perceives
Evidence that supports anxiety
So much wrong but just enough right
Our heroine stands with all her might
Beginning to search for what is her right.

39

Destiny

Unhallowed prayers echo above
Tear drops trickle the uncouth
And yet hearts shatter
And winds whisper
And prayers fall short in the web.

Harsh blows the wind against the plain
Broken bones untouched remain
And yet wine circles
And the brook gurgles
And I am unafraid.

Mercy grows as pain abounds
Cries of a ghost echo all around
And eyes fall shut
And breath disappears
And yet we just stay here.

The Captain again comes into her life
Shuttling the doubts while telling her they
were right
Without doubts you are dumb
A lamb to be slain when the day is done.

 # 40

Peace

They promise peace peace
But all I see
Is an endless sea

They promised joy joy
But all I feel
Is emptiness prevail

They promised ease ease
But each moment my heart stutters
As I struggle to breathe

They promised so many things
But their promises
Were empty.

Their words were simple half the truth
A dangerous measure,
For it is worse

To tell a half truth than a lie
It drowns the senses

And kills the mind.

He promised peace peace
And inside I felt
Perfect peace.

He promised joy joy
And a brook sprung
Raining joy on all inside.

He promised ease ease
And my shoulders found relief
Bearing His great burden of ease.


```
             Puzzle pieces fall in place
         In her joy she dances the night away
         Gone for a minute, the clouding doubt
            Her energy is sudden and loud.
```

 # 41

Puzzles

Puzzle pieces one by one
March in time to the drum
Rat a tat tat it commands
Fairies and folk dance to its dance.

Yahtzee pieces join the fray
Obeying the permission in valiant foray
Rat a tat tat it's voice is true
Keeping tempo for me and you.

But our heroine cannot long be glad
Too many problems and words to be had
So she toys with stupidity
A blindness that will heal agony.

 # 42

Stupidity

The door to heaven
Opens on the east
The door to hell
Cannot be seen

The wind is present
But at what sea?
The galaxy is real
But at which eternity?

The thoughts of another
Are wrapped in mystery
 And yet we consider
The blessing of familiarity.

The world in the dark
Is unknown to most men
Yet we all fear
The darkness within.

The love of a mother
Rivals any love for another

But a child willing leaves
For an embrace of another.

Mysteries hang in the sky above
But we continue to live and love
Our questions are answered too quickly
So we stop asking, embracing stupidity.

```
           But her brain will not let go
              Stupidity is all for show
            It continues on it's mad path
       In the questions that will always be asked
               Lifting the chalice to her lips
         She drains insanity's goblet in one sip.
```

 # 43

Poison Cup

Angel wings are hard to be seen,
Their heartbeats rustle the sea.

Angel tears water the earth
Their salty taste drowning the peace.

Agnostic deities bow the knee
While we simply remain unseen.

Idols line hell's northern shore
Atheists remain evermore.

How does one escape the slippery path
When all pulls towards its hateful path?

Angels sing while we give in
Tasting our poison cup

But unlike the angels we idolize
Our God gives us mercy this time.

Now all around her labels her unstable
Her tears fall and flood the table.

 # 44

Tears

Poison is the preferred taste
Of tears that run in my place
A marathon of hard terrain
The liquid wins as others play.

Tears continue their downward fall
Because our heroine cannot sustain all
The people who need a helping hand
In a world where kindness is banned

 # 45

Symphonies

Innocent as the world may seem
Destruction is at its seams
Death paints a melody
Inspiring departed symphonies

Comedy comes linked with death
It is but a departed breath
And foggy through the glass it seems
Its truth is what we really need.

Despair is not quite the tragedy
That life paints so vividly
Recalling details darkened by time
Reminding me life isn't really mine.

So she recants her caring heart
Giving it to the compost to do it's part
She allows boredom to reign
In the hole she's sustained.

 # 46

Boredom

Boredom creeps like a caterpillar
Inch by inch every further
Into territory yet uncharted
Boredom will not be outsmarted.

Boredom is a bird's eye view
Disinterested in everything but a few
Wings of might bare along
It shushes the nightingale's song.

Boredom is a scepter
A tool not a master
Handle it carefully
For you are it's royalty.

With time to think she has scenes repeat
Of her childhood
An adult she'll quickly be
But she realizes she's never enjoyed
Childhood's sea
Too much piled on her spinning plates
For her to simply live and play.

 # 47

Childhood

Fairies strain to hear these bells
Dryads repel the sensation's quell
All for the magic the notes possess
A child's laughter and innocent bequest

Childhood melts like wax from the mold
Sorrow furrows deep in their soul
Marking adulthood a notch at a time
Fading with childhood's final sign.

Straddled between mermaids and bills
Balancing precariously on it's sill
Some souls grow and others remain
In-between adulthood and childhood's plain.

Death was the one that stole it from her grasp
As they made a friendship that would last
Never far from her sight
Death claimed her friends time after time.

 # 48

Jealousy

Death is jealous of my friends
Stealing them for his dark ends
Whispering promises of the great above
Ripping a hole as he tears what I love.

Death is jealous of my life
God told him that all I own is his prize
But his hands cannot grasp one simple gift
My life is what He will always miss.

Death is jealous of my eyes
Seeing things that mortals
aren't supposed to be see
My eyes remain as my transcendency.

Death is jealous of my abilities
Dancing, joking, smiling in spite of difficulties
His fingers slip as he steals my joy,
Meaning I am still able to employ

Music and melodies that keep him at bay,
Laughter and moonshine that will play

Death is jealous of one simple thing
That in spite of him I have learned to be.

```
              Ever at odds with death and time
           Our heroine continued to search her mind
           Playing with questions that have no truth
                  Writing songs with no tune.
```

49

Oxymorons

What is nothing
The absence of things?
What is something
In the place of everything?

How do we
Comprehend the weak?
How do we
Fight and remain meek?

Oxymorons flout in the sky
Paradoxes stop us from asking why
We assume we have knowledge
But we teeter between hardly acknowledged.

Nothing covers what we see
But our hearts whisper of things
Spiritual and mental lilting tunes
Emotions splatter confusion too

Never worry about the above
You'll die and dissolve just the same

As the ones who care for nothing
Except pleasure and pain.

And when the sun meets the western sky
The worry will melt like the golden sunshine
For regardless of the hour
Something and Nothing remain in power.


```
Just stop.
Two words that push out insanity
Making our heroine wonder if they really see
Or if she's just an inconvenience
So she writes her poetry
For those who want to truly see.
```

50

Childish Feeling

Childish as this feeling may be,
It slithers through my veins,
Tightens around my bones
I will not be free
I will never be home.
Silence is the only gift
I long for in this abyss
But the noise inside matches the noise around
And I know that the music of breath
In this world will always be found.
Glass drips down my cheek
Cutting red rivers in my face
But to you, the noise is simply a sob
The blood is clear and I'm a drama queen
And you won't know the pain
Until I'm gone.
And there's no way to restart the music
Or to play along.

But now pressure continues to mount
She has those she wants to help and those she must
She's loosing count
So pressure steals health in it's climb

51

Hypnos and Thanatos

To the wind my health whispered,
Begging for another breath
My health is a fragile meter
And I am not at its best.

To the tears my soul has registered
Taking in more than its share
To the tears my cup is toasted
And assigned all my cares.

To the death my body is creeping
Its steps halting and swift
Death is just it's final destination
I am waiting at its train station.

To my hopes my heart is fleeting
Begging for unneeded rest
Brothers and kin, two of a kind,
Hypnos and Thanatos continue to decline.

To my mind confusion is creeping
Prisoner to its muddled grasp

Confusion is a master cruelly
Melting matter in its clasp

Fear is not foe or companion
Lungs neither ally or enemy
My existence is by far fleeting
A season in eternity.

```
Perhaps the midpoint of this book has come
 Or maybe the answers did begin to fall
 Needing help doesn't lessen your worth
 If anything, it strengthens your mirth.
```

52

Inspiration

Untaken pills reproach me,
Energy surges through me,
My mind is a Ferris wheel
Each snapshot comes to haunt me
Of events long revealed.

My sleep has forsaken me,
Genius comes to taunt me,
My mind laughs at the midnight hour
As butterflies of inspiration
Flutter by my tower.

Moonlight slides between lace,
Streetlights glimmer in the dim,
My mind finds pictures in the shadows
As angels watch
And the world's whispers begin.

Being a helper may be your life
But boundaries don't always equal strife
Putting bar after bar in place
Our heroine still had kindness in her mental space.

 # 53

Spill the Tea

Please, please tell me your story
Tell me your view on misery
Please, please open your voice
Begin building the past in ice.
Let me learn from your experience
Let me understand you intelligence
Please, please, spill the beans
Give me a cup filled with your tea
Let me take part of your pain
Let me be for you what I need
A friend who care, ears who hear
Someone who will show me the past isn't near.

There is so much in the world she wants to fix
But she was not made the god of the sticks
Allowing help when it's needed
Offering help when she's not beaten

 # 54

End Times

The sky is burning,

My heart is black

Ash is littering

I can't put it back.

The stars are falling,

Star dust burns

Glitter fills emptiness

And I am unworn.

In her own search to find her worth
She found the litter of others on earth
Litter to reuse to shape her outside
Litter that brought joy inside.

 # 55

Litter of Oz

Crimson lips
        Dorothy's shoes
                Whispered I love yous

Burgundy eyes
        Hopeful white lies
                Everything happens in its own way

Haunted voice
        Empty choice
                It's already made for you.

Dimmed dreams
        Unraveling seams
                Don't worry, we'll all leave you

Ghosted smiles
        Deadly wiles
                Whispered I owe yous.

But though there can be some joy inside
Darkness still comes beside
Written in ink black as the soul
Maybe words will help her to grow

56

Mental Stitches

The words won't flow
My mind doesn't know
The ghosts that haunt me.

Prayers offered, tears shed
Can this process be sped
So I can breathe once again?

I have accepted, come clean
I have admitted what I need,
Why must the pain stay?

Mental stitches are being placed,
Mental ions weave into space
But moments pass and I am the same.

Why must my heart continue its beat
Why must my eyes continue to bleed
As God does not pay attention to me?

Glory is beyond my comprehension

Healing is a lie that I can't obtain
God hears my cry and adds more pain.

Loneliness doesn't mean I am alone.
Silence doesn't mean you aren't heard
Your pain might end, your wounds will heal.

The sun will shine, the clouds fly by
The comforts of life, the love gone by
dLife is worth living even if it's a pain.


```
                    But as she opens her mouth
                 He stomps out the flame in one pounce
                    But the scales fall from her eyes
                Religion isn't something he can patronize
                    Someday she'll escape but for now
              She'll write her sword and continue to bow.
```

57

Patriarchy™

Good for you, you broke my soul
Every moment moving towards your goal
Killing the human squirming inside
All for your inevitable design.

Good for you, you've hurt my life
Broken my trust more than twice
Watched me shrivel before your eyes
Yet you've never changed your approach.

Good for you, you rule over me
Breaking my spirit for eternity
Drowning every moment when you can't see
You continue to order what happens inside of me.

Good for you, I can please you
Hiding while I do everything and continue
To die alone behind the scenes
Meeting all of your many needs.

Good for you, spend your hours being holy
Because of you I can barely finish a prayer

My religion shattered before my very eyes
Please tell me this all ends in time.

Good for you, the equation works
Keep tearing others and letting them curse
The actions you take and the decisions you make
Leaving pain in your wake.

Good for you, when are you going to realize
It's so hard for us to love you?
Good for you, when will you see
The reason each one of us is dying?

Good for you, stay in your little world
The future is yet untold
Let us go and we'll change
The world into something you can't recognize
And we'll just smile and say
Good for you.

```
            Burnt and broken, yet so full
         Our heroine still can't empty her load
                Eyes trained only to see
         A maid who's carrying responsibility.
```

58

The Show

My parents don't like me,
Their eyes cannot see
Who I am
Deep down inside of me.

My parents don't know me
They can only know
The me
They want to see and know.

My parents will disown me
If they were not blind
I am not the girl
They love and see inside.

But when her heart is rock hard
Water erodes it away
The tears of a mother
Awakens and saves the day.

59

Diamond Mine

The tears my mother has shed
Due to my life
Could water the ocean
And put out the fuse of strife

The tears I've shed
To be the perfect daughter
Would fill a stream
And provide Africa with water.

Perfect perhaps I cannot be
But my mother doesn't mind
If I'm lacking in that degree
My mother's love is a diamond mine.

Of more value is a mother's love
Than any stone or metal or club
My mother is not perfect you see
But she is more than enough for me.

So with her mother cheering on the sidelines
She steps into the ring armed with rhymes
Pointed towards the needed change
Breaking every one of her chains.

60

Increase

Oppose the proud
Take down the crowd
Their graves a mantra of peace
All will end in decease
So is it the proud that still increase?

Glib though her tongue may be
Our heroine Isn't sure who is she
Is she the one who shrugs out of pain
Or will she continue to internalize it all the same.

 # 61

My Truth

And they say to me
Answering my pleas
Advice to give me ease
So I answer with these

Lines:

"Speak up,
Endure the pain.
Speak louder,
It's all the same.

Don't roll over
Never give in
Don't allow others
To trample your skin.

Stand tall
Make others hear
Don't worry
About the hate that's near

Be yourself
What does that mean?
Speak your truth
Force yourself to be seen."

So I watch
The world take this advice
And maybe all they say
Is actually right.

But for all that,
That's not me.

```
      Internalize it is no longer an option
   People are ruthless, there bleeding and dying
      So she must start rhyming and writing
            To defend, to fight back
            To fill in all of the gap.
```

 # 62

Repeal Its Name

When will Justice
Be blind and yet see?
When will Justice
Prevent the wrongs that be?

When will Justice
Wield its sword?
When will Justice
Allow us to move forward?

When will Justice
Look at you and me?
When will Justice
Listen without heeding prosperity?

When will Justice
Remember that we're the same?
When will Justice
Know that even if we don't share names

We share blood,

We share bonds
We share influence,
We correspond

United our hearts crave
To link arms and face the grave
Our hearts cry the same repeat
For love and kinship and blood.

When will Justice
Unbow its head?
When will Justice
Reveal its name?

When will Justice speak out
And rid us of all this pain?
When will Justice simply say
I am not what you all prayed?

```
          To fix this never ending strife
    Our heroine must define a constant in life
          Love so longed for, so ill at ease
           Love the promise to world peace.
```

 # 63

Love

Without punishment
There is no fear
It is a testament
Of pain endured.

Within love
There is no fear
For love is above
The pain endured.

Love casts out the fear
It covers the pain,
Washes the fevered dream
And binds forgiveness over your name.

Without fear,
There is no safety
Constant alert is near
As if we can prevent morality.

Without love
There is no life

For our hearts need above
Right and wrong, punishment and drugs
A simple compound named love.

Love and punishment
Hand in hand
I rest my case for Justice
To bear her heavy hand.

```
              But as she begins to tamper
             People near start to oppress
        Telling her she'll never know what's best
                  So like a poet of old
            She writes and hides them in a drawer.
```

 # 64

Captivity

Freedom is a promise,
Shame is the answer.
My nest has become my prison,
My watchman has become my tower.

Freedom is vague,
Its bell towers silent
My sanctuary is my dungeon
My guardian is a tyrant.

Liberty is an unspoken word,
Its uniqueness is underrated.
I'll never touch its feathery wings,
I'll never know the harmony it sings.

The prison has become my home,
Its walls my constant trauma
The chains create a melody,
I've fought the familiarity.

But she can't keep the bomb from going
Even if she has no way of knowing
How the public will understand her song
If they'll agree or create a throng
Tar and feathers, fame and praise
Maybe neither, they'll just erase
It won't matter if the match strikes hot
And it lights the fuse.

 # 65

Injustice Fuse

Everything is shot
Fire burning holes
Someone has lit
The injustice fuse.

Hidden for years
Unattended for more
Our anger was led
Right to its door.

Bullets will fly
Others will die
And still the fire creeps
Toward the powder under the news.

Someone has lit
The injustice fuse
The nobodies have hid
The buckets and tools.

Today we stand
Shoulder to shoulder

Our fathers might have been soldiers
But together we'll be something bolder.

Anarchist and hooligans
Creating destruction
At least our aim is true
And our anthem used.

Someone has lit
The injustice fuse
Just pray to God
It won't blow up on you.

```
         As she runs, torch in hand
       She's stopped by the small bands
             All asking to be seen
            For help in life's tragedy
        Instead of becoming a champion
       She hands the torch to each of them
        Showing them how they don't need
           Help from anyone to be free.
```

66

Equality

They cry for help
But we do not give
We claim them pagans
& their blasphemy in amens
But what is the difference
Of our religions?
Despite the fact that they give
And you refuse to see
They cry for help
But all you hear is mutiny.

Black lives matter
Their prayers are loud
You say all lives matter
And ignore the reason they crowd
Black lives matter
Their children wipe tears
Black lives matter
You won't relieve parents' fears.
What is the difference
Between you and them?
Except that their parents were slaves

And you owned them.

Immigrants were your forefathers
No man to force them off the land
Native people held out offerings
Teaching them the ways of the land
But now you keep people from coming
Locking the gates and building walls
You say this country isn't for the taking
When you've already taken it all.
They cry for help, their children dying
You frame them for the fault of it all
Immigrants were your forefathers
But they never had a visa at all.


```
The keys of change are in their hands
 If they stand and begin to understand
Social trust, justice, our generation sees
    And if we begin we'll see change.
```

67

Social Trust

There is a safe that all have keys
To open when they simply please
It's so large all of humanity could happily crowd inside
But instead we all skitter and hide because who wants
Social trust?

There is a thing that all have breathed
Oxygen is a necessity and yet we act as though
It's a nicety painting it in colors of the deepest hue
And ignoring other is our depressing go-to shattering
Social trust.

How can we return to that understanding
Where our children could play without us wondering
Who will steal them off the street, who will murder them in one sweep
And we don't find where it went, but it's disappeared down the vent
Social trust.

Maybe if the world was not all about me
Maybe if I learned to care for all of these

Other humans on this planetary sharing all of the depositories
Maybe then we would have some peace, maybe it would return
Social peace.

Peace is a step right before trust.
Don't worry though, there's no rush
I'm not pushing trust on you an annoying salesman rushing you through
The benefits and the ease your life would take on when you breathe
Social trust.

```
But  even  though  our  heroine  knows  there  will  be
                            change
           She  also  knows  what  others  care  for
           The  fight  for  power,  the  lust  for  peace
```

 # 68

Sad Truth

The only person
Who cares is You
Which is why
The universe makes you choose
Between love and power
Money and peace
A never ending leech
That continues to eat
Even if you never choose.

So she writes to encourage
To push them towards where they need to be
Towards the place we all long to be
Where there truly is equality

69

Canaanland

There is a place
Called Canaanland
Where visas aren't needed
And immigrants aren't banned.

There is a place
Called Canaanland
Where privileged is given
Regardless of your homeland.

There is a place
Far far away
A place where mercy
And justice play.

There is a place
Where your children can roam
A place where you don't worry
About deportation's throne.

There is a place
Called Canaanland

Where all are considered equal
And treated with the same just hand.

So she glares at others as they try to fill
Their sorrow with fulfillment
But the curse of human life
Is to always want or need more.

70

Uniqueness Sea

Fulfillment is a unique thing
Salt to the order of your dream

Fill your hole with cotton and gauze
Blood is no longer the only thing that gnaws.

Anger and hate fill your bones
Marrow replaced for morbid tomes.

Golden suave fills the hole
Promising closure in your soul.

But the scam is just another tool
To destroy just another fool.

To destroy all of humanity
Drowning in the uniqueness sea.

Fulfillment is a unique thing
When a God-sized hole is all you'll ever be.

Should she allow, anxiety would flood
Due to humanity's lust for blood
To understand one's self
You must detour into humanity's wasteland.
Touch those who no one will touch
Those who would be killed in a rush.

 # 71

Humanity

The ray of sun
Burns me to my bone
The teeth of the wind
Sink deep into my tome.

Screaming, screaming
The music trills
Weeping, weeping,
The lyrics kill.

The taste of blood
Chills my tongue
The smell of war
Destroys my nose.

Dying, dying,
Each and everyone
Lying, lying
Cut out your own tongue.

Sun, wind, rain, sky,
Bleach my bones to startling white

Death, dark, light, night,
Nothing instills fear except the right.

> But it's as though none can see
> This world's continual calamity
> They push and pull a heavy weight
> Placing it on our heroine day after day
> She is no more than a hot commodity
> Breaking her soul as they fight for the entirety.

72

People Pleasing

If a robot
Of my mind
Could exist
And save my time
If but I
Was not so kind
Perhaps my people
Wouldn't want my time.
If I could
I'd say no
If I could
I'd share all I know
But I'm the only
Me I know
I'm the only
Amie that grows
Naturally this side of reality
Helping my people
And sharing my time.
But if a robot
Could win their love
I'd give up

The amount I own.

So you still have weight on your head?
You're still balancing on a precipice?
Sliding down the triangle's edge,
Because logic has yet to grant you knowledge?

 # 73

Right Triangle

On
the corners
of geometry the
shapes are built logic
informs every single shade
And the mass is guilt.

Logic
is impossible
Ne'er the easy way
Out a circle, a triangle
diamonds sprinkled throughout.

Think
like a phil-
Osopher explore the
geometry of clouds sprinkle
with insanity whispers of religion's clout.

Expectations on herself
Cause her to put everything on the shelf
Far too much for her to do
Because she has to do everything they choose
Every day it piles on the same

 # 74

Perfect Peace

White fluff flies towards the sky
The eyes look up and reflect the light
Like my soul it seems right.

Our heroine starts to look backwards
Rewatching the past
The past doesn't dictate the future's door
It only gives you direction for what went before.

75

Yesterday's Door

Don't look back
At yesterday's door
It will only
Haunt you all the more.
The past is impossible
To rewrite the script
Is an unachievable feat
To understand the ledgers
Cause madmen to retreat.
But while the past
Is a stoneman's forte
The future and present
Can be rewritten in many ways
The pen is waiting
The stage is set
The only control you have
Is in your own lines
Your actions don't dictate
They only sublime
Influence is key, your major weapon
Influence is better when
Used at your discretion.

Don't look back
At yesterday's door
Look forward to the future
Where you can do so much more.


```
         The future painted in abstract paint
         The expectation in canvas and ink.
        But the peace is still in the process
     Our heroine starting to walk to the future.
```

76

Artist

Red smears
Blue sky
Sitting there wondering why
I can't paint what I visualize.

Soft bristles
White canvas
Millions of ideas
All for the taking if I reach.

Endless mistakes
That's what it takes
To create a masterpiece
And to continue to succeed.

There is uncomfort in with her steps
But she has hope for the future precepts

77

Corset

Laced to uncomfort,
Burning my bones,
My soul is constrained to a pole.

Unopened letters litter,
Taunting my mind,
I'll never know the ink left behind.

Empty words rotate,
Echoing in my soul,
I'll try not to listen to their meanings today.

Love washes tears away,
Heartfelt help comes in some way,
Maybe I'll have to wait to be saved.

But Someday
I'll no longer feel this way.

Seasons comes out to play
And our girl tries to spend time and stay
They say outside lessons anxiety
Spring comes, it changes her life
But she'll miss winter and its cold strife.

78

King Frost

Sunflowers smile on all today
The leaves drop decorating the floor
Our wind whispers, we don't know what it says
But Fall has come to stay.

Allergies triggered as animals whisper
Knowing winter is on its way
Laughter scatters like the litter
Left on Halloween last.

Mellow the sky as it prepares the storm
That will tear life from the branches
Smiles are brief before the chill seeps
Stealing the joy from the bones.

Fall is displaced.

The world has so many ups and downs
So many variables floating round and round
Our heroine finds there is no formula
The hurdles life brings mixes with expectancy
Creating a million things
That wish to drown our queen
But the formulas to break
Can also make
Someone full of strength

 # 79

Chemistry

Without passion, Life is tame.
Without chaos, any king could reign
Without peace, the grave is king
Without emotion, nothing would sing.

Elements on Life's periodic table
Creating compounds as important as metal
Twirling elements into crystal
Importance shades impassive and gradual.

Without freedom, all is lost
Without heartache, love isn't a cross
Without darkness, we have no light
Without emptiness, we would survive.

Elements on Life's periodic table
Mixing into something others call unstable
My words tangle intimately creating love
Your eyes jump, missing all the meanings above.

And even though it doesn't have to be
She studies everyone's identity
To find the very best way
To make them smile every day.

 # 80

Love Language

A simple kiss
A proud smile
Words that affirm
And add a thousand more miles.

A love outside my grasp
A punishment waiting to snap
The moment I try to love
To give what I can of my time

I know I'm not ready
For someone else to love
I know I'm too empty
To give like the one above.

But I want to be one
Of the small percent
That doesn't live to regret.

To regret the love given
Or received
To regret the words spoken

Or unspoken in peace.

I want to whisper
To shout and scream
To make a difference
And be loved, you see.

                    Love a tool, she will forever prize
                    Life still throws her a surprise

 # 81

Pop!

Pop!
The air is
No longer in the tube

Pop!
Life is gone
From me to use.

Pop!
Air will keep
But so will me.

Pop!
Just continue
To breathe.

A surprise scented full of summer
Telling her the coming of another
   Year is right on the verge
   So she squashes the urge.

82

Perfume

A single scent
Sunshine on earth
A small hint
Of beauty in me.

A little drop
Of magic and life
Perhaps that's all that's
Worthwhile in life.

The promise of new life
Breaks rusted chains
Ten months of sixteen have gone
And she is no longer the same.

 # 83

Just A Name

Wind adds emotion
Sun continues its motion
The scent of spring
Complete unity brings.

Warmth adds memory
Birds display dignity
The weeds grow unheard
And souls are undone.

Singles grow in their aloneness
Couples closer grow in devotedness
While birds build their nests
And the dead enjoy eternal rest.

Newness crowns Mother Nature
Glory shrouds the Creator
As green appears again
And life is on the mend.

Begin again, rise before
Grow and flourish all the more

As our relationships change
And spring is more than just a name.

```
            Written to her unknown lover
            Written to the one she'll find
           She's finally open to the prospect
    She finally thinks her burdens aren't too heavy
```

 # 84

Birdsong to You

Airelle shift to cosmic gloom
All the minutes I spend away from you

A sun to my galaxy sky
Can you please tell me why

My soul cleaves to our unity
Fearing your inevitable leave

Time stands still when you're alone
Your taste causes my throat to close

A fear of you tightens my soul
Your eyes water me to my toes

Never leave my soul empty
For without you, where would I go?

A moon to my midnight daze,
Your words continue to stay

Wrap me in your gentle arms

And do not turn me from your charms.

I am yours, and yet I know
You're a phantom I'll never really know.

```
           So she looks into the window
               Of every passing soul
           Hoping to drop a bit of wisdom
              Even if they don't know.
```

 # 85

Window

The eyes that peer deep
Can reveal what they see
Is it a window
Or a prison beneath
A fringe of lashes protecting the seam.

A color of bronze strengthens
The gaze of amusement
Transcends its ways
Is it a shield to keep bullets away
Or is it a sword to open my brain?

What is the soul that looks into mine?
What is the emotion that garbs his mind?
What is the question deep inside?
Is his connection just like mine?

It came from the girl armed with a pen
Who believed in a world bigger than them
A world where all will be right
In its time.

86

Paradise

In a wolf den
Bleats a lamb
Teeth hidden
Peace therein

A leopard cleans
A kid's young coat
The bleating copies
The rumbling throat.

A calf dances
With the Lion
Large shadows playing
And mysteries flying.

Eden whispers a glimpse
As the predator whispers
The lamb answers
And Eden glimmers.

From the top
The shoot appears

But it stays and
Brings the root near.

Eden, Eden,
Our tears still fall
But the root of Jesse
Will wipe them all.


```
            A world where women no longer fear
              Where they're equal on every tier
        A world where the forgotten, hurt, and maimed
           Find wholeness and identity just the same.
```

 # 87

Women

Anne Frank wrote a diary
And I write poetry
Anne Frank's life ended
And mine is just beginning
Yet I feel a kinship with her mind
Both of us are women of our time.

Harriet Tubman saved her people
I write to save them too
Harriet Tubman died a savior
I have yet to live to that tune
Yet I feel a kinship with her heart
Both of us are women who want to give others a start.

Florence Nightingale broke expectations
I write to do the same
Florence Nightingale inserted stitches
In a nation of division intense
I have never made a difference
Yet I feel a kinship with her hands
Both of us are women who want to stitch the gaps.

Women in history have marched before
My sights on them as I continue through the door
Perhaps I'll be blessed and be lined with them
Or perhaps at best I'll just be near the floor
Looking up at the women who changed my life
The women who have sacrificed.

```
      She moved to work like an adult
   Our heroine learning a lot about all
      She wrote and saw and sang and knew
       In the hard labor she went through.
```

88

Boba, my Doll

I have worked since I was thirteen
The paychecks buying what I need
But I didn't realize the truth
Work is what I needed to make it through.

Boba, my doll, you have come to my aid
You have melted through my exterior
And taken its place.

Boba, my doll, you have taught my life lessons
You have pushed me past who I thought I was
And filled me into the person I love.

I have worked since I was thirteen
It wasn't a requirement it was just a thing
The money was enough but don't you see?
Hard work is a good thing.

So she writes poetry dedicated to you
But in the lines she finds what's true
She's not a poet, a one sided dimension
She's a person with multifaceted ambitions.

89

Poetry

I started the story with
I don't know me
Now shall I end
With an introductory?

I am a woman with a brain and time
I am creative, a dragon's mine
I am chosen, a daughter of a king
I am the person that I want to be.

Sure I have moments when I cannot breathe
Sure I have moments when all I want to do is end me
But I have come quite a long way
Sometimes it feels like a journey and others a page change.

I am a optimist raised by a pessimist
I am a dreamer, an opportunity chaser
I am elastic, bound to bounce back
I am Amie, and that is that.

No more do I hate the mirror I see

No longer do I not know me.
Poetry is a lifelong pursuit
Maybe one day it'll iron my suit.

Until I come to that miraculous discovery
I'll just continue being me.
The pen a scribble with my melodies
And I will smile because this is how I know me.


```
       The seventeenth year approaches faster and
                           faster
        Her final few weeks of the dreadful hour
         Reminds her why she survived this year
          Hope in the heart and eyes on the goal
          Our heroine enters for one last show.
```

90

Hot Air

Hope is hot air in my wings
Chance is my buoyancy
No longer has sickness chained me
I will melt into the next year with brilliancy.

Hope is sunshine on my skin
The heat kissing the blood within
Bleeding is no longer my curse
I've grown and pushed past the pain inert.

Hope is powdered sugar on my tongue
Comfort like a blanket made of fluff
My clouds will never melt, the static's enough
Blow the candles, making my wish with ease.

Bowing as the curtains close
Blowing kisses to the souls that chose
To be apart of the journey
Toasts given as the new year reviewed
All the best to Seventeen
And the future to use.

91

Goodbye

The last page of a notebook
The end of an age
The last streak of a pen
Writing your name

Good things end with sadness
Bad things end with happiness
But at times things end
And all you feel is emptiness.

Bittersweet it sticks to your teeth
Lasting too long for you to taste
Never ending, the ends remain
As you finish writing your name.

Note from the Author

The heroine of our story is written to be an inspiration not only for you, dear reader, but for myself. This book is written for you, for all of you who are buckling under the pressure and the weight that has fallen on your shoulders. But it's also written for me, to remind me of the lesson I learned when I was sixteen.

I learned to cope. A lot of time, we hear the world coping, and link it with negative words, but in my case, it wasn't negative, it wasn't positive. It just was.

A lot of living just is. You spend your life doing the next best thing, and do you know that is? It's pouring love into others while saving some for yourself.

I learned that individuating yourself isn't telling those around you that you hate them. It's simply telling them where you begin and where they end. The world wouldn't be an exciting place if there wasn't self expression and unique people.

Lastly, I learned to love fully and freely, without the anxiety of being hurt holding me back. We'll be hurt in life, to be loved will result in pain, but it also results in a life well lived and an existence well used.

Keep living that life well.

All the hearts,

Amie

Acknowledgements

It's time to tell you who's actually to receive credit for this lovely book in your hands! A huge thanks to my editor and one of my sweetest friends, Charis Rae. She caught all the mistakes and made sure this book is 100% pristine for your reading pleasure.

A huge shout-out to my closest friend and my actual sister, Ruth Woleslagle, for saving my behind and doing the illustrations. I think we can all agree she did a beautiful job.

I'm so thankful for all the people who have helped get the word out about Sixteen, and the people invested in my poetry. Keep on changing the world, beautiful beings.

I need to thank my family for putting up with me during the highs and lows of my years. Especially the lows, when I become a grumpy and irritable elf. You guys continue to inspire me every day, and I'll always be thankful.

Lastly, and most importantly, I need to thank YOU! For picking up this book, for letting this dream lifestyle become a reality for me.

All the hearts,

Amie

*"Life with this darkness seems too long,
It grows into a dense throng
My mind can't shake it,
My heart can't take it."*

Want more of Amie's poetry? Read her first compilation!

About the Author

Amie Woleslagle is the author of *Fifteen*, a poetry compilation from a teen to other teens struggling with mental health. Currently a student at The Author Conservatory, she has big dreams for her future career. When she isn't working on creating worlds and writing both poetry and prose, she's painting books for her business, Painted Prose Designs, singing broadway songs on the top of her lungs, or cuddling her furry pets. She dwells in the Peach State, where the weather is hardly ever too cold, and mostly too hot. You can join her wild adventures on her IG @writingamieanne or follow her newsletter (amiewoleslagle.com).

www.ingramcontent.com/pod-product-compliance
Lightning Source LLC
Chambersburg PA
CBHW072051110526
44590CB00018B/3128